Published by:

Kistel Media
Jacksonville, Florida
www.KistelMedia.com

KISTEL MEDIA

TISIRI

ISBN: 978-0-9891719-1-5

Hello land-lovers!

My name is Spike, and I am a tugboat. Normally tugboats like me are busy working on the waterway, but I am a little different. I am a home for fish and sea critters. Read along to learn how this came to be.

Once upon a time,

a long time ago, I was busy working like other tugboats. My job was to push barges up and down the river, and I was really good at it.

One day, I broke down
and was taken out of the water to sit
on dry land. I was no longer able to
work on the waterways. I was so upset
because I didn't think I was going to be
able to do anything anymore!

I decided I wanted to help

the environment, and I imagined myself as an artificial reef. Artificial reefs are formed from large pieces of clean metal or concrete that are placed in the ocean. These structures create homes and food for animals such as fish, crabs, and corals. Since my body is made of metal I was perfect for the job!

I had a lot to do

before I could become a home for fish. I had to make sure I was clean and safe before I was placed in the ocean. Several people helped with the preparation process and often used tools on me to remove certain parts...OUCH!

Ok, it didn't hurt, but I was a little nervous about it.   These parts would not be good for sea life so they just had to go.

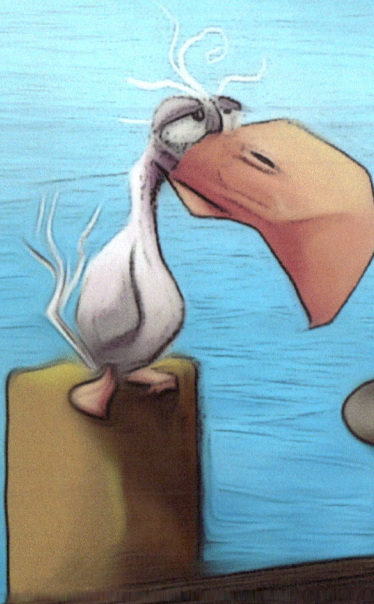

15

All that preparation made me lose 140,000 pounds! Take a look at

BEFORE

my before and after pictures. I was now half my original weight.

AFTER

Being lighter sure made things a little easier for Mr.

Crane as he lifted me and put me back in the water.

It sure felt good

to be back on the water even though this time I was being pushed by another tug boat. I was excited!   I was on my way out to sea heading towards my new home.

Once out to sea,

I was detached from my escort tug and filled with water. I was slowly sinking!

Eventually, I became so heavy with water

that I sank below the surface to the seafloor.

It sure seemed weird

being underwater for the first time, but I was now at my new home.

A few weeks later

I started to make friends with fish and sea creatures that wanted to make me their home.

I was actually beginning to grow "hair" of all things! This "hair" was really algae and barnacles that had begun to grow on me.

Today, I have been underwater for quite some time and I am a thriving reef! My "hair" has thickened; now it consists of corals and sponges as well as barnacles and algae. Funny thing is that my fish and

marine critter friends like my hair. They actually nibble on it for snacks and it provides them additional shelter. Word has spread about all this snacking so I am now filled with fish and marine life galore. Take a look at all my new friends!

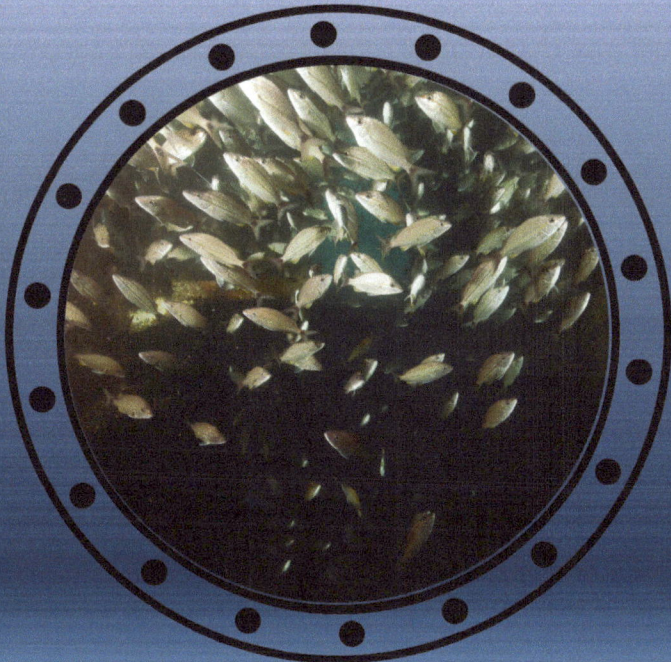

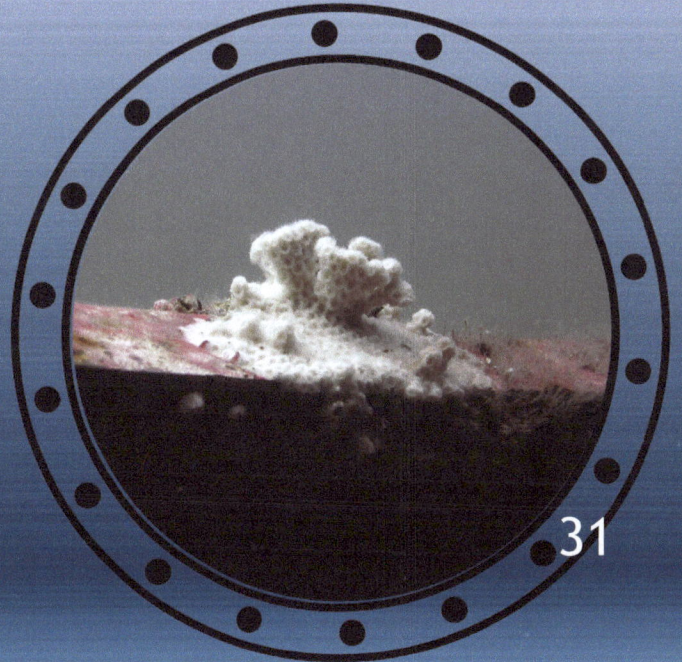

THE END

Author:
Joseph Kistel

Spike Illustrations:
Ali Pordeli

Contributers:
Jolene Roszel
Larry Davis (underwater images p. 30)
Keith Millie "FWC" (underwater image p. 27)

Special Thanks:
Ed Kalakauskis, Safe Harbor Maritime Academy, United States Coast Guard Sector Jacksonville, W.W. Gay, City of Jacksonville, Florida Fish and Wildlife Conservation Commission (FWC), Jacksonville Offshore Sports Fishing Club, Jacksonville Reef Research Team, Jacksonville Fire and Rescue, Jacksonville Police Department, Naval Station Mayport, Nassau WebDesign, Earth Day Jacksonville, Vistakon

www.ingramcontent.com/pod-product-compliance
Lightning Source LLC
Chambersburg PA
CBHW042003100426
42813CB00020B/2967